# Self-Confidence: The Entrepreneur's 30-Day Roadmap to Building Self-Confidence & Overcoming Self-Doubt

by Ben Gothard

CEO & Founder of Gothard Enterprises LLC

Author of CEO at 20: A Little Book for Big Dreams

# CONFIDENCE

*"With confidence, you can reach truly amazing heights; without confidence, even the simplest accomplishments are beyond your grasp." - Dr. Jim Loehr Ed. D., Author, Psychologist & Entrepreneur*

Do you, or someone you know, have an incredible amount of potential but lack the self-confidence to take action? If so, you are not alone. Everyone has natural talents and gifts: some are brilliant financiers, others are cunning linguists, and certain people are incredible entrepreneurs. However, not everyone makes the most of their strengths. There are countless reasons why people do not take advantage of their natural abilities, but not having confidence is the most common. In any area of your life, especially business and entrepreneurship, confidence determines your success, both in degree and longevity. While the value of passion, a strong work ethic, and a proper mindset cannot be overstated, the degree to which you rely on yourself will dictate how much you can accomplish. In this book, you will not only gain a new understanding of and appreciation for confidence, but you will also be given the tools to improve yourself through my unique 30-day challenge.

# CHAPTER 1: WHAT IS CONFIDENCE?

*"It is confidence in our bodies, minds, and spirits that allows us to keep looking for new adventures." - Oprah Winfrey*

## Confidence is Belief

Confidence is a modern idea with a historic root. The word "confidence" comes from the Latin phrase 'confides,' which translates to 'with faith.' Confidence, at its core, is the capacity to have faith in yourself and your abilities.

When you are confident, you trust in your skills, intuition, and ability to achieve your goals. Rather than being dependent on others, you rely on your own judgment. To be confident is to believe, beyond all doubt, that you can and will succeed.

Confident thinking is not a novel concept. Successful people attribute their success to confidence in addition to talent and luck. Legendary basketball player Michael Jordan, for example, is a man who has demonstrated the power of belief time and time again. In high school, Jordan was cut from the varsity team during his sophomore year, but, instead of getting discouraged, he remained positive and determined. He continued to train, practice, and hone his skills as a basketball player. Because of his unwavering belief in himself, he made the varsity team the next year and went on to play at the University of North Carolina under a basketball scholarship. In 1982, his first year of college, Jordan was named Rookie of the Year and his team won the NCAA championship. After being named college player of the year for the next two seasons, he was picked up by the Chicago

Bulls in the 1984 NBA draft and was part of the Summer 1984 United States Olympic basketball team that won the gold medal. Fast-forward to 1993, and Jordan had already won three straight NBA titles, three regular season and playoff MVP awards, and seven straight scoring titles.

Despite his incredible success, Jordan's life changed irrevocably in that summer of 1993 when his father was murdered. Because of this tragedy, he retired from professional basketball soon after.

But a man of such resilience and indestructible confidence cannot be dissuaded from his dreams, and Jordan rejoined the league for the 1994-95 season after a seventeen-month hiatus from basketball.

The world questioned him when he returned to the professional basketball scene, but his faith in his own talent surpassed any doubt. After losing in the playoffs in his first season back, Jordan led the Bulls to their fourth NBA title in the 1995-96 season. The final game was played on Father's Day, the three-year anniversary of his father's horrific murder. From that moment, Jordan went on to win a fifth and sixth NBA title and solidify his spot in history.

If Jordan had not been able to carry on in spite of rejection and personal turmoil, he would not have fulfilled his destiny to be one of the greatest (if not THE greatest) players to have ever played the game of basketball. If he had given up as a sophomore in high school, nobody would know who Michael Jordan is today. You, like myself, probably do not have the athletic ability to be the next MJ, but you *do* have innate gifts that make you who you are. Harness them with confidence, and believe in yourself, because if you don't, then nobody else will.

## Confidence is Action

Katty Kay, author of *The Confidence Code*, claims that "confidence is life's enabler – it is the quality that turns thoughts into action." Confidence is not just belief in yourself, but constant, deliberate action through that belief. The good news is that confidence has an exponential growth rate, meaning that the more assertive action you take, the more confident you become. You just need to take that first step.

You might be thinking, "well that's not helpful because I'm not confident enough to take that first step, that's why I got this book!" Luckily, the 30-day challenge in Chapter 3 will give you the tools to build the confidence you need to take the first step. But in the meantime, I want to share the story of James Dyson with you. You may recognize his last name from your vacuum cleaner. Dyson, now a billionaire engineer, did not find success immediately. In fact, he failed quite a few times. In an interview with Matthew Kirdahy of Forbes in 2008, Dyson said:

> I spent about five or six years developing a completely different kind of vacuum cleaner. I built over 5,000 prototypes to get the system to work. Every year I was getting further and further into debt. In the end, I owed something like $4 million. I took out two or three mortgages on my house. If I failed, everything I owned would've gone to the bank. Everybody thought I was completely mad. [As it turned out] I repaid the bank loan

within about four or five months of first selling the product. The bank kept using me in their advertising as an example of how they loan money.

I want to emphasize that I am absolutely NOT saying to go $4 million in debt. I wanted to share his story with you to reiterate that confidence is a crucial component to success. There is nothing distinguishable you and him; he simply believed in himself and took constant, deliberate action to make him dreams a reality.

## How Are Confidence & Courage Related?

To have confidence is to have conviction in your abilities and take action through that belief, but what is courage? Aren't they the same thing?

I am no expert in courage, so I want to cite Eric Kaufmann, a brilliant author, speaker and corporate coach. In his TED Talk, Kaufmann describes the experience of quitting his job, donating all of his worldly possessions, building a cabin in the woods, and devoting himself to spiritual practice that he had been practicing for the past ten years. He expected this process to be a spiritual awakening, but he did not anticipate the intensity with which he was going to have to face his fears. First came a fear of failure, the fear that he was going to fail in his personal and professional endeavors. He worried that others would find out he was not as strong or smart as he wanted people to believe. These feelings ultimately boiled down to a deep-rooted fear that he was fundamentally unworthy of success or happiness. Isolated and depressed, his thoughts of worthlessness consumed him to the point that he concluded the only solution was to kill himself. As he recollects, that idea was "truly terrifying," but he survived with courage.

Courage, as defined by Kaufmann, is "deliberately walking towards what you'd rather walk away from." Like confidence, courage can be cultivated and is just as much a part of us as fear. In fact, building a relationship with your fear through Kaufmann's method is one of our steps to develop courage.

In his talk, he proposes three steps when confronting fear: Feel, Face, and Embrace. Instead of avoiding fear, you must experience it, not just by recognizing that you are scared, but also by taking note of its effect on your body and spirit. Let it grip you and allow it to exist without trying to deny it. Once you feel your fear, pause, and then take three deep breaths. When you make an effort to stop your thoughts, you give yourself space. This space provides an opportunity for choice: either you let the fear chase you or you chase it. Once you make the decision to accept fear, then you can face it by labeling it. Kaufmann states, "As soon as you can name something, you can deal with it." Instead of letting fear be your master, you are choosing to be its partner. The final step is to walk towards the fear and confront it head on by making a plan. Your plan is not focused on eliminating fear, but learning to live with it. When you face that which you dread head on and master your reaction to fear, you cultivate courage.

On a side note, my Uncle Eric didn't commit suicide. He is a great mentor, friend and beloved part of my family. I am grateful to be so close to someone of his caliber, and his book, *The Four Virtues of a Leader: Navigating the Hero's Journey*

*Through Risk to Results,* is a brilliant, visionary guide to developing leadership. But I digress.

Whereas confidence is belief in yourself and action through that belief, courage is taking deliberate action in spite of fear or uncertainty. Confidence leads to courage, since you need to be strong enough to act when you would prefer not to. I also think that in some cases, you need to have the courage to take that first step in building self-confidence. For now, let's leave it at a chicken and egg scenario.

## What About Self-Esteem?

Now that we have discussed confidence and courage, where does self-esteem fit into the equation? Many people use confidence and self-esteem interchangeably, but these two qualities are different. While confidence is the belief in your talents and abilities, it can also be skill specific. For example, I think I'm a decent basketball player and have confidence in my abilities to shoot a ball, but I cannot draw a picture to save my life. This is not a reflection of a lack of confidence in general, but the realization that I haven't put enough time developing my artistic ability.

On the other hand, self-esteem is a measurement of your own value in the world. If you answer the question, "Am I a worthwhile person" with a resounding "Yes," you probably have good self-esteem and vice versa. Self-esteem doesn't vary from skill to skill. If you have high self-esteem in one area of your life, you probably have it in another because, as Katty Kay points out, it is "a reflection of how you see yourself."

## Confidence vs. Overconfidence

Whereas a healthy amount of confidence is necessary to chase your dreams in life, overconfidence is a surefire method to have those same dreams quickly vanish from sight.

As you develop confidence, as with anything, staying humble is essential. Overconfidence can lead to reckless decision-making that may halt your journey to success in its tracks, particularly if you are an entrepreneur. Business involves dealing with people in many different capacities. Being confident when you interact with others is crucial, but being cocky is a HUGE turnoff. The stark contrast between confidence and overconfidence is that the former allows you to maintain a realistic view of yourself and understand where you need to improve, while overconfident individuals overestimate themselves and often refuse to accept that they don't know everything.

In my time as an entrepreneur and author, for example, I constantly walk the line between confidence and overconfidence. I have to be bold enough to put my products and work out there and persevere through harsh criticism (of which there is plenty), while at the same time be humble enough to accept help when it is offered. I attribute a large part of my success in life (limited though it may be) to the constructive criticism of mentors to whom I put my trust, and I strongly encourage you to find some of your own.

Regardless of how effective the roadmap in this book is for building your confidence, it is up to you to remain connected to, and respectful of, other people as you continue your journey.

# CHAPTER 2: WHY DO I NEED CONFIDENCE?

*"You can have anything you want if you are willing to give up the belief that you can't have it." - Dr. Robert Anthony, Psychotherapist*

If you want to succeed in life, you need to be confident that you can and will reach your goals. Because your ability to take deliberate action is a crucial piece of accomplishing meaningful objectives, developing confidence is a critical aspect of life. You need it!

## To Seize Opportunity

When an opportunity presents itself, a confident individual takes advantage of it as opposed to letting it slip through his or her grasp. Without confidence, you are not able to act. The people who are confident in their ability to succeed will take risks that others will not and with great risk comes great reward. When you take risks, there will always be the possibility of failure, but not trying at all guarantees failure.

The great Albert Einstein put it best when he said, "A ship is always safe at the shore – but that is NOT what it was built for." You are always safe when you don't take risks, but you will never find out how much you could have accomplished if you do not try. I'm not much of a believer in a pre-determined destiny. I believe that we choose our own fate through the decisions that we make. When you see a chance to better your situation, take it. If you have the opportunity to succeed, then go for it.

Granted, I'm not saying that you should say "yes" to everything. That may lead you down different paths that are not the most efficient use of your time and effort. Instead, make decisions with confidence. Understand what you can and need to do, push away everything else, and pursue the goals that you set with confidence.

## To Learn & Grow

As your confidence grows, boundaries will disappear. Inexperience and lack of knowledge will not stop you from moving forward, only present a new challenge to overcome. With confidence, you know that you can always learn new things in your life and nothing will stop you. With confidence, you are free to take action in your life.

Imagine that you are a new chef who doesn't know too many recipes. Instead of accepting the fact that you "don't know how to do that," you could see each unknown recipe as a unique challenge to be conquered. Slowly, but surely, you can build up a repertoire of recipes and eventually start making your own recipes. Nobody can take that hard-earned knowledge away from you and with each accomplishment your confidence will grow.

## To Be Unstoppable

Failure does not deter confidence. Rather, it is an opportunity for learning and growth. The ability to conquer failure is a powerful tool to expand your skillset, overcome obstacles, and become unstoppable.

Thomas Edison, for example, tried thousands of

prototypes for the electric light bulb before he found the combination of parts and pieces that worked. On his experiences, he said, "I have not failed. I've just found 10,000 ways that won't work." To put it another way, if you fall down 10 times, get up 11. When you keep pushing despite repeated failure, you are unstoppable. You only face true failure when you give up.

### But Does Confidence Benefit Entrepreneurs?

When you are an entrepreneur, the confidence to believe in yourself and take action on that belief determines whether you succeed or fail. Let's look at a couple people who, without confidence, would not have been able to get where they are today.

### Jeff Bezos

Many entrepreneurs have historically cited "big names" like Steve Jobs, Bill Gates, and Elon Musk as people they look up to in the tech business world, and Jeff Bezos, Founder & CEO of Amazon.com, is just as wildly successful and brilliant. His inspiring story will hopefully motivate you to be more confident.

Intelligent and skilled from a young age, Bezos graduated summa cum laude from Princeton University in computer science and electrical engineering. From there, he began a lucrative, yet short, career on Wall Street. Throughout the next few years, Bezos got the entrepreneur's bug: he wanted to create something. And in February of 1994, he found just what he had been searching for. After watching the Internet grow by 2,300% in just one year, he had the idea of "the everything store." He left Wall Street behind, started his journey, and never looked back.

Bezos encountered many obstacles while he built Amazon.com, but remained confident in his vision to create the behemoth we know today. Bezos has said, "If you're not stubborn, you'll give up on experiments too soon. And if you're not flexible, you'll pound your head against the wall and you won't see a different solution to a problem you're trying to solve." You can see his obstinacy in Amazon's volume over profit approach to business. Instead of focusing on making profit, Bezos simply grows his business by investing every penny back into the business. It has been frequently criticized and questioned, but Amazon's annual revenue has jumped from $48.08 billion in 2011 to over $100 billion in 2015. The numbers speak for themselves.

While he constantly works to perfect his craft, Bezos never doubts his vision. After testing, he pivots and learns from failed concepts, in order to reach the next success quickly. Many of the major design elements that seem innate to his business, such as Amazon Prime or super saver shipping for example, resulted from unsuccessful experiments that he learned from. But he always keeps his "big picture" in mind and pursues it relentlessly. The efficiency and creativity with which Bezos works is incredible and would not be possible unless he had confidence in himself and his ability to perform under pressure. You must commit to being fully confident in your own endeavors, but, like Bezos, willing to learn from unsuccessful ideas. He *knew* he had something amazing to offer the world and did not stop until he brought it to life. He was rigid in his vision of "the everything store," but flexible in how he developed it. You have something amazing to offer the world, too. Do not stop until you see it realized.

## Arianna Huffington

In 2005, Huffington created The Huffington Post, now one of the most widely read news sources on the Internet. When she was just sixteen, she moved from her home in Greece to Cambridge, England in order to study Economics. For several decades, before moving to the United States, she wrote and published political and biographical books, among others. Her name only first started to be recognized in relation to her husband Michael Huffington, who was a member of the United States House of Representatives, but it was not until after their divorce in 1997 that she began to gain notoriety for her own ideas and accomplishments.

A few years after creating her own successful column online, Huffington founded The Huffington Post in 2005. This big break did not come until she was in her mid-fifties, following years of work, effort and repeated failure. Because of her conviction in her work and her resolve to accomplish what she set her mind to, she has been on *Time* magazine's and *Forbes* Top 100 lists for Most Influential People and Women. Huffington sold the still tremendously popular blogging website to AOL in 2011 for over $300 million. Numbers talk.

Huffington's resilience and determination to continuously strive for success is rooted in confidence, and without it, she would not have gotten where she is today. She, like every successful person before her, has experienced repeated failure to go alongside her enormous success: "We need to accept that we won't always make the right decisions, that we'll screw up royally sometimes – understanding that failure is not the opposite of success, it's part of success."

As you continue on your journey, keep in mind what these two self-starters have experienced and accomplished. Their failures paved the path to their success. Nothing can stop you if you are confident that you can and will accomplish what you want and take deliberate action to pursue your dreams.

# CHAPTER 3: HOW DO I BUILD CONFIDENCE?

*"Low self-confidence isn't a life sentence. Self-confidence can be learned, practiced, and mastered--just like any other skill. Once you master it, everything in your life will change for the better." - Barrie Davenport, Author and life coach*

## The Power of 30 Days

There is a reason why I want you to commit yourself to personal development using my 30-day method: it works. Elise from Slothstorm.com puts it best, "30 days is ideal for committing yourself to a daily challenge, because it's a long enough period of time for you to develop good habits and see progress, but short enough that it's not completely overwhelming or never ending."

In one month, you are never too far from the end, and your goal is always in sight. If you pursue your goal, in this case confidence, with the belief that you will succeed and follow the steps provided, you will start to develop confidence and rid yourself of a few bad habits along the way. Through consistent effort, you will achieve small goals every day, and these will culminate to help you build long-lasting confidence.

## Start With the Right Mindset – Keep Your Expectations Realistic

If you take this 30-day challenge seriously, you will begin to see positive changes in your life. At the end of the month, you will have a strong foundation for genuine confidence, and your goals won't be as far-fetched. You will know how to be confident.

However, none of this can happen without dedication on your part. You have to put forth time and effort into the challenge and follow the tasks I have outlined. There may be times you want to quit or your motivation will falter. If you notice this, ask yourself if the short-term work is worth enjoying the benefits for the rest of your life. The fruits of your labor this next month will pay dividends for the rest of your life. Let's begin.

## Day 1: Write A 'Brag Letter'

Dr. Ivan Joseph, Director of Athletics at Ryerson University, in his TED talk, describes the power of writing a brag letter. During a period of insecurity in his life, the simple act of writing down and then re-reading a list of his personal and professional achievements helped to preserve his self-confidence.

Today, you are going to write yourself a brag letter. Begin with,

"Dear [Your Name], This is a letter to remind you of everything awesome you have done so far in your life."

List everything you have ever done that has made you proud to be you. This should include educational achievements, professional accomplishments, fulfilling friendships, skills that you have honed, a healthy romantic relationship you have developed, funny stories that you are a part of, and anything else that makes you feel good about yourself. Do not be coy or humble, it is called a brag letter for a reason. Nobody else has to read this, so don't hold anything back.

Once you have finished writing, keep a copy of it on hand at all times. You can keep a copy on your phone, print out a multiple copies to put on your walls at home, tuck it away in your wallet, or leave it on your office desk. If you are ever in need of a confidence boost, read your letter again, and get focused again. You have more to achieve.

**Be confident in your past.**

---

## Day 2: Write Down Your Goals

I promise, the entire 30 days will not be entirely focused on writing, but this second exercise is just as important as the first. Whereas yesterday you are recalling past success, today is about self-reflection and goal setting. Take a moment to honestly evaluate yourself by answering these questions. What am I good at? Where do I need improvement?

The first task for today is to write down 5 strengths and weaknesses that you have. Self-reflection is hard, especially at the level that will cause meaningful, positive change in your life. However, the rewards are much greater and longer lasting than the discomfort needed to understand yourself.

The second task for today is to write down the two biggest goals that you have in your professional and personal life (4 goals in total), two being being long-term and two short-term. These long-term goals aren't small objectives, like losing a few pounds. They are your "if I were to achieve this my life would be set" goals; they should reflect your purpose, or at least what you think your purpose may be at this time. If you are struggling to think of good goals to choose, try to work on your strengths and weaknesses. If you are a strong communicator and mathematician, consider creating a YouTube channel where you teach math and aim to hit 1,000,000 subscribers. If you are a skilled artist and love to travel, maybe you could start a blog where you create art in different parts of the world and try to visit 100 different countries.

By writing your goals down, you make them tangible. You are giving yourself a concrete target to aim for, with both short and long term success clearly defined. Write this in a place where you will see it every day. Personally, I set an alarm on my phone for 3PM every single day with the same message on it. Your goals are what get you out of bed in the morning.

**Be confident in your goals.**

---

## Day 3: Share The Load

Once you have your goals in front of you, share them with a trusted friend or family member. Pick someone who could benefit from a confidence boost and is willing to 'check in' with you once a week. During each check-in, both of you should share what you have done to improve since you spoke last. You might even want to take this 30-day challenge together.

When you have somebody else to hold you accountable for staying focused, and you them, the likelihood of *not* achieving success starts to seem almost impossible. This is a tough step to take, because once you vocalize your intentions to another, you establish an expectation. However, this step can be the difference between seeing this challenge through or not. If you start losing motivation at any point in the next 27 days, your trusted friend or family member will help you get back on track. Just remember, you should extend your encouragement and support back to them as often and as best as you can. Make your collective journey about teamwork and fulfillment.

## Be confident in your support system.

**Lagniappe:** I have always admired people who declare their goals publically on YouTube or any other social media platform because they are putting themselves out there for the world to see. But here's the big secret: when you proclaim your intentions to those around you, the people who are aligned with that goal will *want* you to succeed. That's right. You will find supporters, some of whom you may not have even known before. When you give people a reason to root for you, you are actively leading by example. You are a role model for positive change.

If you find that you don't have anyone to turn to for a support system, I would love for you to reach out! I can help you stay focused on your goal, but if you need more encouragement, you can also join an elite network of entrepreneurs, authors and incredible people that I'm building on Facebook who can help you stay motivated along the way. I stand by the words in this book, and I encourage you to take me up on this offer. Please reach out to me at bgothard@gothardpreneur.com. But I digress.

## Day 4: Dress to Impress

How you present yourself to the outside world is important. Writer and marketer Natalie Jobity, MBA, said, "Your appearance is your expression to others about who you are and what you stand for." Your ability to keep yourself groomed and cared for reflects your self-worth, confidence, and state of mind. Maintain a strong visual presence, and you feel better about yourself.

Today, you are going to shower and shave; spend time not just cleaning, but taking care of yourself. Do something you would only do for a special occasion, whether that means painting your nails or putting on cologne. Dress like the person who you want to be. Spend as much time as you need, then look at yourself in the mirror. *I bet you look pretty damn good!* You are a strong, confident person, and now your appearance tells the same story. Whenever you dress like the person you want to be, you are preparing every part of yourself to become that successful, and eventually you will be. You are only going to make more progress from here, so keep up the good work.

### Be confident in your appearance.

---

## Day 5: Make Eye Contact

This one is difficult, I know. Intense social interaction, especially with strangers, can be a little intimidating. However, the best way to get past this is to practice.

Today, all you need to do is look people in the eyes. While this is simple in theory, it is hard to maintain when people start looking back. Nevertheless, confident individuals are not afraid to connect with others in meaningful ways, so you must challenge yourself to hold steady eye contact.

Interestingly enough, when you start looking others in the eyes, you'll probably notice something peculiar: *they can't hold your gaze.* Lack of confidence is rampant, and even at this early stage of confidence development, you'll start noticing a difference between yourself and the overwhelming majority of people who are still at square one.

**Be confident in your ability to connect with others.**

---

## Day 6: Do One Good Deed

Having confidence in yourself is easier when you are a good person because you have integrity and can take solace in the fact that you are always trying to do the right thing. Lying, manipulating, and flaking out on responsibility is easy to do in the short-term, but will deteriorate your relationship with yourself and others in the long run. Because you are striving to do the right thing, you don't have to be ashamed of who you are. Quite the opposite, you should be proud of who you are and confident in your actions.

Today, be generous without expectation of recognition or reward. Do something good just to do it: donate your time or money to charity, buy a coffee for the person behind you in line, give someone a genuine compliment, or help someone move. Once you do this one good deed, you will notice how easy and fun it will be to do another. Acts of random kindness can come back to help you in many different ways. First and foremost, you are getting out of your own head. This 30-day challenge is an intense month of self-examination, purposeful action, and personal growth. Take this day to put your problems in perspective by helping somebody out. By uplifting others, you vicariously bring yourself up too.

**Be confident in your ability to help others.**

---

## Day 7: Clean Your Desk

Being organized is a great way to get things done, both on a small and large scale. While your desk is a small part of your life, it is something that you have complete control over. When the world around you is chaotic, you can take solace in a clean desk. As Leo Babauta, author and blogger, puts it, a clean desk "is the calm in the center of the storm around me."

**Today, I want you to clean your desk in three easy steps:**

1. Take every piece of paper you have out of your desk and pile it all into your new "Intake" space. This space is where everything must pass before it makes it into or onto your desk.
2. Sort through every single piece of paper and either throw it away, delegate it to someone else, file it away, or handle it if you can get it done within 5 minutes.
3. Maintain this system as you go about your day for all new pieces of paper and once a day for all of your paper.

**Be confident in your workspace.**

---

## Day 8: Gratitude Is Key

I cannot stress enough the importance of dismissing negative thoughts and choosing to think differently. Negative thoughts are intrusive, but you can choose to listen or not. I'm not saying to sugarcoat your life. The world isn't perfect and you may not be exactly where you want to be in life right now. Instead, your goal is to replace negativity with something better: gratitude.

Today, whenever you start thinking negatively, make a mental list of ten things for which you are thankful. Nothing is too small or too silly to be included in your list. I typically think of how grateful I am for my incredible family and my golden retriever, Phoebe. By staving off negativity and introducing gratitude to your system, you are mastering your own thoughts. You are choosing to put your mind in a good place. Not many people have that power. There will be more tactics to further rid yourself of negativity later in the challenge. For now though…

**Be confident in the mastery of your own thoughts.**

## Day 9: Make a "Pump Up" music playlist

Have you ever felt emotional changes in response to certain music? According to the National Association for Music Education, the psychology of music is substantial, and listening to music can improve your creativity and happiness and even decrease anxiety. Many athletes, performers, and even business people use music before big events to energize and motivate themselves to perform at maximum capacity.

Today's challenge is to make a playlist of at least twenty-five songs that make you feel empowered and confident. Don't be embarrassed to include any music that you want on this playlist. Your music choice is personal, and this is YOUR playlist. If a song makes you feel unstoppable and gets you pumped, include it. Keep this playlist on hand for those times when your self-esteem needs a boost in the right direction. I highly recommend starting every morning with this playlist. As you go through your morning routine, use this power packed list of songs to get in the zone for the day.

**Be confident in your music.**

---

### Day 10: Make use of positive images

We human beings are visual creatures. What we see around us has an enormous impact on our mood, outlook, and perception of ourselves. You need to make sure that you are surrounding yourself with positivity. Today, try to incorporate positive images into your life. Take a look at the list below and try at least one of the following:

- Find an inspirational quote or image about self-confidence online, and make it your wallpaper on your phone or computer.
- Cut out motivational pictures from magazines or print something out from the Internet. Tape what you've collected to your wall or put it somewhere you can see it.
- Find some photos that make you happy, like pictures with friends and family on vacation. Frame them, and look at these photos for a confidence boost.

Let these positive images uplift you every time you look

at them. You are a third of the way there.

**Be confident in your use of positive images.**

---

## Day 11: Exercise

Your exercise for this day is exactly that, *exercise*. I want you to get up and do something. Think about different activities or sports that you are good at and enjoy doing. Then, go do it. Getting your heart rate up and working up a sweat is not only healthy, but can be extremely empowering. This month is focused on your mental health, but you can't neglect your physical health in this month either. Instead of wasting energy worrying or stressing about things in life that you can't control, invest that energy in a healthier way. Go work out or ride a bike or play a sport. Put your negative thoughts aside, get out of your head, and break a sweat.

Exercise is physically healthy for you, and it can dramatically improve your confidence, too. By finding your physical prowess in a certain activity and working towards mastery of your skills in that one capacity, you are going to improve. By improving your skills through constant effort, you are building your competence and confidence in that one area. This confidence will spill over into other aspects of your life.

**Be confident in your physical ability.**

---

## Day 12: Find A Mentor

If you have struggled in your life, you know that listening

to people who bring you down is a waste of valuable time and energy. I want you to find people who will inspire you to be better. I want you to find mentors who can guide you to success.

Today, strategically write down 5 people who you would like to have as mentors. Find people who you want to be like in the next year, two years, five years, ten years, and twenty plus years. These people can be as apparently unreachable as Mark Cuban or as near to you as your high school English teacher. The idea here is to find guidance for every step of your life. Whereas your two-year mentor can give you short-term advice, your twenty or more year mentor can help you keep the big picture in mind.

Before your 30-day challenge is over, reach out to these people any way you can. Personally, I think that social media is a phenomenal place to identify and connect with potential mentors. For example, I am a big fan of Dale L. Roberts. He is a best-selling author, Kindle Publishing expert, and puts up YouTube videos teaching and inspiring others to follow in his footsteps. I was so moved by his words that I reached out to him on social media asking if he would be interested in chatting, and he actually agreed to let me interview him. It was like a dream come true.

**Be confident in those who guide you.**

---

## Day 13: Teach Something

Think about all the things you know, and then narrow it down to what you understand particularly well. Your goal is to identify something that you do better than most people.

Today, I want you to record a video of yourself teaching something. It doesn't matter what it is that you're teaching or who you are trying to teach. You could pass on life advice, answer a question you think people may have on a certain topic, or teach a lesson. What matters is that you are providing knowledge to someone else.

One of the greatest gifts you can give the world is your knowledge and experience. Passing on information you've gathered from educating yourself and gathering experience to another person is a great way to boost your own confidence. When you teach someone something worthwhile, you have the opportunity to improve his or her life. When you help someone through your teachings, you are accomplishing a few things. First, you are building competency in your ability to pass along information. Second, you are affirming that your knowledge and experience is valuable to somebody else who isn't as far along in that particular area as you. Finally, you are expanding your circle of influence in a positive way. The more people you help, the more respect you will garner.

**Be confident in your ability to teach.**

On a side note, if this is something that you truly enjoy, you might want to consider uploading your video to YouTube or building an online course. Anyone who has that particular problem can turn to you as a resource, and you might even make a few dollars in the process.

---

**Day 14: Learn to re-frame a negative situation**

"There is nothing either good or bad but thinking makes it so" is a famous quote from *Hamlet*. We cannot always control what happens to us in life, but we can control how we deal with it. When you reframe a situation to see it in a positive light, it will become a lot more manageable. When you can see the good in every situation, your ability to handle whatever life throws at you dramatically improves.

Today, take a new look at a negative situation that has been bothering you and change your perspective. Reframe your "problem" as a "challenge." This simple mindset change will make your obstacles a little less intimidating. Mark Twain once said, "My life has been filled with terrible misfortunes, most of which never happened." A problem, or in Twain's case a misfortune, is simply an inefficient way to view your circumstance.

For example, suppose that you are currently living with your parents because you are between jobs or places. You may have thoughts like, "It's embarrassing to be living with my parents" or "I can't see a way out of my situation." By making an active choice to reframe the situation, healthier and more positive thoughts will emerge. For example, "It's not ideal, but at least I can save up some money" and "I get the chance to get to know my parents as adults." The way you think about a situation is entirely based on your perspective and removing any negativity will help you fix whatever is bothering you.

Don't spend another minute thinking about how hard your life is. Fill your mind with enthusiasm at all of the exciting challenges you have to face and the opportunity for growth you will have from overcoming them.

**Be confident in your ability to find perspective.**

## Day 15: Practice Power Poses

This challenge is a physical one, but you'll benefit from it mentally as well. I'm not an expert on posture, but I have been dealing with lower back pain for years now, so I can offer some tips to make you more comfortable. When you have pain on your mind, it is hard to think of anything else, much less developing confidence. Take pressure off of your lower back in three easy steps:

1. Find a flat wall and stand up straight with your back against the wall and legs together.
2. With your hand, feel the space between your lower back and the wall; there should be a slight curvature or arch.
3. Deliberately decrease that space, and feel the pressure release from your back.

Rinse and repeat this process until your posture permanently reflects this lessening of the arch in your lower back. You can also start practicing the following positions:

### Power Pose

- Stand with legs wide apart and hands on your hips
- Place your hands on a table in front of you with a strong lower stance
- Smile, and smile big
- Keep your palms and arms open, instead of closing yourself off
- Don't stop smiling, but continue on with your day after 5 to 10 minutes

### Resting Pose

- Go to a flat wall where you have some space
- Position yourself where your back is on the ground and your legs are up on the wall
- Rest for 20 minutes in the position
- Refer to the picture below to check your form!

Get these movements into your muscle memory and into practice at your home or wherever you feel comfortable. When you feel comfortable, rested and powerful, it is a lot easier to focus on building your confidence.

**Be confident in your ability to find comfort and relieve stress.**

---

### Day 16: Stop Listening to Yourself & Start Talking to Yourself

Imagine if you had somebody following you around all day, degrading everything you said, did, and thought. Some of you may already have people in your life that take on that role for you. It can be mentally damaging to constantly hear things like "You'll never get it right" or "What made you think this would be a good idea?" or "Nothing works out, so why bother?" This negativity erodes confidence; yet, you probably tolerate this kind of treatment from yourself. A criticizing voice in your head is more influential than others; don't let it be more vicious than others, too.

Today, I want you to talk to yourself more than you listen to yourself. For the entirety of today, talk to yourself like the champion you are. Give yourself credit for the good things you do (like a coach praises a good catch) and figure out what you can learn from any mistakes. You could even write down any negative thoughts on a piece of paper, then tear it up and throw the pieces in the trash. Give it your best effort for 24 hours, and you will be blown away by the results. Is it weird to talk to yourself? Maybe. But if it works, then who cares?

**Be confident in your ability to communicate with yourself.**

---

### Day 17: Start being inspired by others

Do you often catch yourself comparing your life to the lives of other people? We all do it at some point, but it can eat away at your confidence if you don't do it correctly. There will always be someone richer, smarter, faster, and more accomplished than you. When you happen across people who are more successful than you, direct comparison isn't the answer. Instead, I want you to find inspiration in and take lessons from the achievements of others.

Today, do research on five notable people in your field (or people who have already accomplished goals similar to yours). Listen to their stories and take note of how and why they did what they did. By following in the footsteps of others, you are giving yourself many paths to success. You don't need to reinvent the wheel. I often find that TEDX talks are motivational and informative. The objective is to find people who are smarter than you to learn from and let their stories build your confidence as you continue on your journey.

**Be confident in your ability to be inspired by others.**

---

## Day 18: Sit in a quiet room and face down your fears

As my Uncle Eric explained in his TED talk, we all experience fear throughout our lives. The mistake many of us make is that we try to distract ourselves from feelings of fear rather than face them directly. Today, you are going to follow in his footsteps and literally sit with your fears.

Turn off your phone and other devices for a few hours. Find a quiet, comfortable place with zero distractions. You are simply going to sit alone and see what thoughts and feelings your mind throws at you. Like my uncle, you will probably find that all kinds of insecurities and worries surface. Watch them, observe them, but do not engage. Notice that when you allow yourself to feel fear and the associated physical sensations, there is no need to run. Live with your anxieties as they come up. Ask "why" you are afraid of each individual fear and write them down on a piece of paper. Labeling your fears gives you the power to understand and conquer them. Refer back to my Uncle Eric's method of Fear, Face and Embrace if you are struggling to overcome this task.

**Be confident in your ability to face your fears.**

---

## Day 19: Work out what a confident person would do, and do it

Leo Gura of Actualized.org recommends thinking on an 'as if' basis when building your confidence, and I agree wholeheartedly. Sometimes you need to "fake it till you make it." Psychology is a powerful and effective way to train yourself. When you operate like a confidently, you will see the results of confident actions. Over time, you will naturally start believing in these actions and eventually, develop greater confidence.

Today, your task is to tackle one specific fear you wrote down yesterday. Your goal is to understand exactly what causes you so much distress, and then decide what someone with a high level of confidence would do to address it.

For example, suppose you become anxious when giving a presentation at work. What elements of that situation cause you to become nervous? Is it a fear of public speaking? Is it a feeling of inadequacy among your peer group? Is it a sense of impending failure with no other option? Break it down as far as possible. When you have identified these specific points, write them down.

The next step is to work out what a confident person – or a confident version of you – would do differently. For instance, you may decide that a confident person would acknowledge that failure is an option, but as long as you keep getting back up and give it your best shot, it is never permanent. According to Leo Gura, this step informs how you should try and behave in future – acknowledge that you are afraid, but then make a conscious choice to behave differently. Fake it until you make it. It may feel forced at first, but you will be surprised at how natural your new behaviors become.

**Be confident in your ability to take action.**

---

## Day 20: Start visualizing a more confident future

Visualization is an incredibly powerful tool. This challenge follows up on Day 2, in which you came up with your goals.

Today, I want you to take this one step further. Revisit your self-evaluation and goals that you set on Day 2. Re-evaluate your strengths and weaknesses and set new goals or improve old your ones to reflect your transformation this month. Consider the individual progress you have made thus far on your goals. Picture yourself using your newfound confidence to meet these objectives. Top athletes commonly use visualization for a good reason: it sets up expectations for your brain and mind to follow. Think about how you will move, how you will talk, and how you will handle any setbacks. See yourself happy and proud once you get there and remind yourself that it feels wonderful to be so confident and in control of your life.

**Be confident in your progress.**

## Day 21: Speak with more authority

People who speak in a rushed voice tend to be less confident and credible than those who take their time. Your challenge today may seem simple, but it will have a significant effect on the way others perceive you and the way you see yourself.

Today, you are going to speak at 75% of your normal pace, taking extra time to think about what you are going to say and how you are going to say it before you let the words flow.

When you slow down both in responding and speaking, you have time to process more information. When you put more thought into what you are saying, the ideas you express will be communicated with greater sincerity and confidence. You will command more respect and authority by slowing down because it conveys that what you have to say is worthwhile and helpful.

**Be confident in your ability to speak with authority.**

## Day 22: Achieve a goal within a day

Most of your life goals are going to be medium or long-term in nature. Getting a degree, building a business, or having a great relationship doesn't happen overnight. These things take time, effort, and an accumulation of a critical mass of short-term goals. Short-term goals are crucial for two reasons. First, they are stepping-stones to larger goals. You aren't going to be able to write an incredible book, for example, in one day. Trust me, I've tried. Instead, you could write an amazing sentence. Then another. Soon, you'll have a paragraph. Then another. See where I'm going with this? Accomplishing large tasks is not a random occurrence; it is the product of completing a critical mass of small tasks. You do not win a war at once; you must win a number of battles first.

Second, setting and achieving a small goal is a fantastic way to increase your confidence. Once you finish your first paragraph, for example, you will realize that it wasn't that hard to do. If you're like me, you'll develop an insatiable hunger for another paragraph, and another. In making tangible progress within a short span of time, you prove to yourself that you are capable of accomplishment. This repetition of small success will grow over time.

Today's challenge is to pick a goal or challenge that will take you a few hours to conquer but will help you accomplish your larger goals. For example, you could set a goal to write an article, to learn how to use a new piece of software, to set up a basic blog for your business, or to establish an e-mail connection with five leaders in your field. Whatever the goal is, make sure it is relevant to your broader goal and take action immediately.

**Be confident in your ability to achieve goals.**

---

## Day 23: Ask a trusted friend for an honest evaluation

Confident people look to themselves first and foremost for confirmation. They know that they can take pride in who they are, and they do not depend on others to for self-esteem. People who are confident AND smart, however, get advice from other people who are more knowledgeable and experienced than they are.

Remember Day 2 when you evaluated your strengths and weaknesses and Day 20 when you re-evaluated? Today, you are going to talk to a trusted friend or mentor and ask them to give you an honest, objective evaluation on the same qualities and traits you judged yourself on. The goal is to get constructive criticism on your abilities in order to improve your natural gifts.

It will be interesting for you to see the difference in your own self-evaluation from Day 2 to Day 20, and then see what other people think on the same topic. Use this evaluation to understand and start working on your weaknesses and remain confident in your strengths.

**Be confident in your external evaluation.**

---

## Day 24: Start breaking a bad habit

If you are a slave to self-destructive tendencies, it's hard to fully believe in yourself. Today, you are going to start breaking a bad habit. We all have them – whether it's smoking, drinking, staying up too late, or watching too many hours of TV. Breaking these habits is important for two reasons: first, when you are spending time on these bad habits, you are taking time away from chasing your dreams. We only have a certain amount of time in our lives to devote to our goals. Don't let a bad habit inhibit you. Second, by parting ways with negative tendencies, you are proving to yourself that you don't need those things to be successful. You can rely on yourself. You are allowing yourself to have confidence in your own abilities.

Today, I want you to pick one of your bad habits and draw up a plan to defeat it. For instance, you may have fallen into the habit of going to bed at 1am and know that you need two more hours of sleep to be fully rested. Your plan could be to bring your bedtime forward by half an hour per week, then another half hour next week, and so on until you start going to bed at a more reasonable time every night. As long as you take small steps towards big goals, you can overcome any bad habits that you face.

To be sure, I am suggesting that you tackle one bad habit at a time. It is tempting to try and do a complete 180 and change every bad habit you have all at once, but this is an unrealistic expectation. Give yourself time to change and have confidence that a positive step every day IS ENOUGH to make meaningful change in your life.

**Be confident in your ability to make meaningful change.**

---

## Day 25: Volunteer

On Day 6, your challenge was to do one good deed. Today's challenge takes this one step further. I want you to volunteer for a charitable cause and give something back to the community that you are a part of. This month has been filled with intense personal growth. Instead of spending time on yourself today, you are putting the needs of others first. By focusing on problems greater than your own, you will find it much easier to put your own troubles into perspective.

You may have a busy schedule and not be able to volunteer on a regular basis. If this is your situation, try to contribute a little bit of time throughout the year. Make it clear to the organization you choose that you are not in a position to help out regularly, but you will contribute a few hours when you can. Do not underestimate the importance of this day. When you choose to impact the lives of others, you prove that your actions can cause meaningful change. Once you realize that, you can confidently create positive change in your own life.

**Be confident in your ability to impact your own life and the lives of those around you.**

## Day 26: Stop being a perfectionist

Before you immediately close this book and discard my advice, hear me out on this one. When you are a perfectionist in every area of your life, you are setting unrealistic expectations for yourself. If you fail to reach every goal that you set, there is no way to keep your confidence at a healthy level.

Today, I want you to dispel your current notion of perfectionism and embrace a mindset of perpetual improvement through a three-step process:

1. Accept your imperfection
2. Seek constructive feedback
3. Improve & Repeat

For example, let's say you are building a product. Instead of spending two years on development, spend 6 months, put that product out to market for 3 months, get feedback, and improve, then rinse and repeat. To be sure, I am not suggesting that you put out low quality work or hold yourself to a low standard. Rather, I'm suggesting that once you hit a professional or personal ceiling, accept your imperfection rather than view it as a failure. Get feedback, make improvements, and keep plugging along until you hit another ceiling.

By spending too much time trying to find perfection in every aspect of your life, you are delaying opportunities for growth.

**Be confident in your imperfection and your ability to improve.**

---

## Day 27: Be a leader

A hallmark of confident people is their inclination to assume leadership positions. Leadership forces you to put the needs of your constituents before your own.

Today's challenge is to put yourself in a leadership position. This doesn't necessarily mean applying for a new job or starting your own business – the challenges below are enough to get the taste of leadership:

- Plan a social get-together. If you are like most people who lack confidence, you probably wait for someone else to suggest lunch, drinks, or other activities. This time, you are going to be that person. Send out a group message or Facebook invite. You could even start a regular meet-up, like lunch with your colleagues every Tuesday.

- Put yourself forward for additional responsibility in your job. If you know that someone needs to be responsible for organizing a new training program or a conference at work, why not volunteer yourself?

- Start a movement. For instance, if your neighborhood needs cleaner water, why not consider setting up a community group that organizes river rinses?

When you put yourself in a leadership position, you are allowing yourself to grow as an individual and take pride in your development. When you see the fruits of your labor, your confidence will swell.

**Be confident in your ability to lead.**

---

## Day 28: Get creative

Creativity is a fundamental trait in our society. Creative people are the agents of change to any community. Unfortunately, many people mistakenly believe that only some people are born to be creative and that creativity is static. This is a fallacy. Everyone has the capacity to be more creative, especially entrepreneurs and innovators!

Today's challenge is to prove to yourself that you have the gift of creativity and take confidence in that fact. Set aside an hour today in which you dedicate yourself entirely to a creative pursuit. You don't have to paint a picture or sculpt a vase if you don't want to. Instead, try one or more of the creative activities listed below or choose your own:

- Make a list of 5 brand-new solutions to an ongoing problem you have been facing, even if they are a little wacky or 'off the wall.' This is especially helpful if you can solve a business-related problem you have been wrestling with for a while.
- Write a 10-line Acrostic poem about confidence and

your development journey thus far. The first line should start with C, the second with O, and so on.

- Look around your home or office. Can you find an unwanted object that is just crying out to be re-used or 'up cycled'? Make an art project out of it!

- Load up a few of your favorite photos on your computer. Using image-editing software, add some amusing captions, make some memes, or create a photo collage to share with your friends or family.

- In an ideal world, where would you like to live? What would your ideal home be like? Create a mood board, complete with sketches, colors and images. Make your vision come alive.

**Be confident in your ability to be creative.**

---

### Day 29: Build up the confidence of another person

By now, you should realize that building confidence is not just about yourself. Your challenges these past days have been difficult, and today, you get to pay it forward.

Today's exercise involves helping somebody else build confidence. Give compliments, help others, or support those who need it. Taking small, deliberate action to raise others up can make an enormous difference to those who are down. After 28 days of hard work, you know how difficult it is to raise your own confidence and how grateful you would have been if someone reached out to you to help. Like I've said before, when you are a positive force in others' lives, it gives you perspective on your own circumstances. Take note of their level of confidence. You were probably there not too long ago.

**Be confident in your ability to build confidence in yourself and others.**

---

### Day 30: Lay down on the street for 30 seconds

Coach, speaker and founder of Comfort Zone Crusher Till H. Groß gave an inspiring TEDX talk on overcoming fear and social anxiety. Like you, he challenged himself to get outside of his comfort zone. He wanted to prove to himself that disapproval from other people wasn't the end of the world. You are going to do the same thing.

Your challenge today is to lie down in a public place, like a street corner, for at least 30 seconds (don't be afraid to stay there for as long as you need to overcome any anxiety you may have). Even if you don't do any other challenge in this program, try this one. I personally guarantee that you will see results.

**Be confident in yourself and your journey. You made it.**

---

### A Quick Word

Congratulations! You ought to feel very proud of yourself for facing your fears and taking these steps to develop your confidence. Well done!

If you took this 30-day challenge seriously, I want to hear your story and your results with my program. Reach me here. I would love to hear from you and, if you're interested, interview you for my YouTube channel dedicated to

Entrepreneurship and Self-Help. Again, **I want to interview you**! Your story can be an inspiration to others who are in need of confidence.

# FINAL THOUGHTS

*"If you are insecure, guess what? The rest of the world is, too. Do not overestimate the competition and underestimate yourself. You are better than you think." - T. Harv Eker, Entrepreneur and motivational speaker*

By now, you should have completed the 30-day challenge and feel more confident. You are just as worthy of success and respect as everyone else, and I hope you are excited to pursue your dreams with renewed vigor and genuine confidence.

Without faith in yourself, you cannot realistically achieve your goals and get where you want to be in life. Only when you surrender your ego and decide to improve yourself can you hope to make your dreams come true.

If you completed all the challenges to the fullest and worked hard to improve yourself during these 30 days, the changes have already begun to occur. Don't panic if you don't feel any major shifts in yourself or your life just yet. It takes time to see results.

Confidence is a lifelong project. There will always be difficult situations to overcome, and all too often, you will encounter people and situations that have the potential to chip away at you. Place yourself and your confidence first, and repeat the program as many times as you need. Occasionally, you may find yourself slipping back into old ways of thinking. This is not a failure – old habits die hard. The trick is to be proactive in maintaining your confidence and consistently make progress. And who knows, you still might have some fun along the way!

Made in the USA
Coppell, TX
01 December 2021